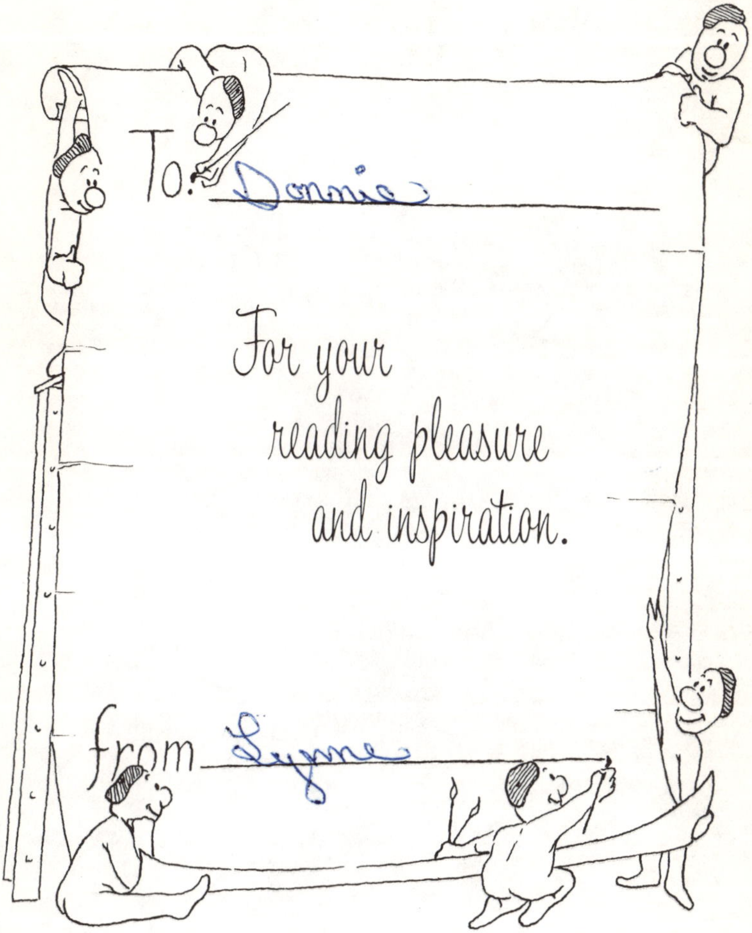

To: Donnie

For your reading pleasure and inspiration.

from Lynne

If The Shoe Fits...!

By
Harry and Joan Mier

Editor:
GILBERT READE

Associate Editor:
JOHN M. KELLER

Cartoonist:
DON W. JACOBS

Merit Publishers, Beverly Hills, California

BY HARRY AND JOAN MIER

If The Shoe Fits
Happiness Begins Before Breakfast
Building Our Own Rainbows

Ninth Printing, 1969

© 1958, 1967, by Harry and Joan Mier. *All rights reserved, including the right of reproduction in whole or in part in any form, except for short quotations in critical essays and reviews.*

MANUFACTURED IN THE UNITED STATES OF AMERICA.

Contents

FOREWORD — 1

PART I — 3
The World Is Your Mirror

PART II — 47
Making Strides

PART III — 101
Count Yourself In

Acknowledgment

For their special assistance in the preparation of this volume, the authors thank Mrs. Maxwell Fields, Mr. David Gelb, Mr. J. B. Handley, Mr. Jack B. Mier and Mr. Walter Usher.

Foreword

There is a deeply warm and human quality in the observations on life which Joan and Harry Mier have stated so simply in their aptly-entitled volume, "If The Shoe Fits . . . !"

Here is confirmation of many of our own viewpoints, and of some we recognize as belonging to people we know and love. Here, too, are reminders of past experiences. In these thoughts we find strengthening of faith — in God, in ourselves and in our fellow-man. Ancient truths begin to glow anew as enduring signposts for guidance and offer a lift to our spirits.

The Miers' comments and reflections comprise an often witty and always compassionate approach for casting into proper perspective the frustrations and pressures which beset our daily lives.

These varied thoughts, consciously applied in daily living, can increase our understanding and consideration of others, brighten our outlook on life, and enable us to draw from it the richest rewards and satisfactions.

*Friendship is a worthy craft
Of noble, pure design
Carved by four willing hands —
Yours, my friend, and mine.*

*All good wishes.
Joan and Harry Mier*

PART I

THE WORLD IS YOUR MIRROR

THE WORLD IS YOUR MIRROR

Laugh, and laughter ripples back,
Cry, and tears surround you;
Smile, and the world will smile;
Frown—and you'll find frowns, too.

The cheerful "hello" will echo back,
An unkind word brings only gloom.
A happy face warms the atmosphere,
But, the cold shoulder chills a room.

Decide what it is you'd like from life,
For, as you live, so the world appears—
Live and act the part yourself:
The world reflects your smiles or tears!

FOR A FULLER LIFE

Declare
A new independence
Of mind and heart;
Throw off
The bonds of tedium,
The chains of habit,
The oppression
Of unnecessary pressures:
Liberate
Your time and your energies
For concentration
On those areas of life
Which are
The most meaningful to you
And, so
The most rewarding.

FOURTH-DIMENSION

Cherish the visions of your mind,
Preserve the ideals of your spirit,
Remember the music of inspiration
That stirs in your heart.
For an idea,
Born in the mind
And nurtured in the heart,
Raised in the dimension of dreams,
Will, with the spur and guidance
Of determination and effort,
Emerge at maturity
Into the realm of reality.

The World Is Your Mirror

SPECIALIST

Will we trust to maintain
Our plane's repair
One who's never made
A kite to fly?
Or expect to learn
Cultivation of grain
From one whose fields
All barren lie?
So, to learn right answers
To questions we pose,
Should we not ask them
Of one who knows?

AT THE READY

Although might
Isn't always right,
Victory belongs
To the brave and strong.
For even a cause that's just
Will fall to dust
If they won't fight
Who believe its right.

IN ONE EAR...!

It is better to let some things
Go in one ear and out the other,
Than to let them go
In one ear and out the mouth!

If The Shoe Fits

GOSSIP JUNGLE

Some social error or
An unguarded remark
To the holocaust of gossip
May set incendiary spark.

Like jackals and vultures,
Gossips over rumor drool;
They enlarge and abort it
Into a murderous tool.

Wicked tongues spread
The poison of defamation,
Sorely wounding the victim,
Smearing reputation.

With chickens home to roost,
When the worm has turned,
Malicious scandal-mongers
Get the treatment earned!

INANE INCENTIVES

It's not so much
The things we need
For which we'll strive
And sometimes bleed,
But for those extra frills
Like the Joneses have
That we'll go in hock—
Mere "ego-salve."

The World Is Your Mirror

FORFEITED BOND

A commitment that is made
But whose fulfillment is delayed
Too long after it's been spoken
Has the value of a promise broken.
Loneliness one day will give cause to grieve
To one whose word others cease to believe.

MISSING LINK

Sometimes the goals we seek
Remain out of reach
Only because we fail
To extend our hand to grasp them!

DEPOSED

She charged mental cruelty
That he'd sorely neglected her —
When actually he'd been working
So long and hard to support her.

On alimony she's now living high,
While he's left poor and alone;
And some other guy's enjoying luxury
While occupying his old throne.

If The Shoe Fits

BAT AND BALL

There's a personality conflict
Whenever they meet;
With words, each will try
The other to defeat.

The repartee gets personal,
It's tit-for-tat;
When one starts pitching
The other goes to bat.

Spectators are wearied
By the heated "sport"—
This battle of sharp words
And fiery retort.

Their friends would be happier
If a truce they'd call—
If they'd lay down the bat
And toss away the ball!

CEREBRAL NAVIGATION

While our hearts
May be the inspiring force,
It's best that our heads
Be charting our course.

The World Is Your Mirror

MATURATION

How desperately some cling
To their material things,
Like some willful little boy
To a favorite little toy.

They don't seem, or want, to know
That little boys must grow,
And must then give the boot
To their infantile pursuit.

Then only will they feel
Satisfaction that is real,
That is not to their senses tied,
But, rather, to what they sense inside.

SCAPEGOAT

Of their plans, some seek your approval
For which they'll applaud you as wise;
But if such sours or turns out badly
They'll blame the failure on your "advice."

A REAL TEST

One of man's greatest
Tests of strength
Is the will to correct
His own weaknesses.

9

If The Shoe Fits

TAKING THINGS FOR GRANTED

Many things in our lives
We just take for granted,
Accepting motives and deeds
In a manner off-handed.
In business, in society,
And in other ways,
We go naively and trustingly
Through the days.

However able and honest
Things or people appear,
There's a margin for error
That can be costly and dear.
Those we're relying on
May be doing it, too —
Taking things for granted
The same as we do.

Remember the responsibility
That rests on your neck,
And on things affecting you
Keep a knowing check.
Really seeing and thinking
Is to live the safe way;
Taking things for granted
May cost you all someday!

JUST ANOTHER LITTLE RIPPLE

Don't be discouraged
By another's overnight success:
Many things which make a big splash
Quickly sink to the bottom.

The World Is Your Mirror

THE CRITIC

It seems that too frequently
Those who criticize most
Are those least qualified
To damn or to toast.

They usually lack experience,
And have not all the facts
Regarding whatever subject
Exposed to their attacks.

But intelligent criticism
Is constructive and fair,
With suggested improvements
Based on thought and care.

INVESTIGATE

Before helping one who seems
Stuck in the mud,
Stop and think a minute;
Make sure he's really mired
And wants your help,
And not just wallowing in it.

LOSING STREAK

One who will not heed
The lessons of defeat
Will find that like disasters
Will endlessly repeat.

If The Shoe Fits

THROWING WEIGHT AROUND

Many a worthwhile project
Has failed or run aground
Because some little tyrant
Threw his weight around.

An unbecoming mantle
Authority may be—
When placed on shoulders
Unused to responsibility.

Authority's insignia
Proper courtesy will merit
When this respect is earned
By those who wear it!

HANDLE WITH CARE

Fragile
Are the silken strands
Of the web of human love;
And often,
Once shattered,
They can never be rewoven.

BURNED BRIDGES

Sometimes the cutting off
Of all avenues of retreat
Is the most effective incentive
To advance.

The World Is Your Mirror

SOME SOOTHING BALM

When another's thoughtless ways
Make us feel hurt—or even cry,
Let's be thankful that these ways
Are theirs, not ours, to live by.

BULL IN THE CHINA SHOP

Have you ever met the
"Bull in the china shop,"
One who upsets everything
From bottom to top?

Such persons seem to
Hurtle through life,
Always stampeding,
Spreading riot and strife.

These "bulls" never assess
The damage they've wrought,
And haven't a care for the
Unhappiness brought.

If you encounter this "bull,"
Step aside or you're next
On the list of china shops
About to be wrecked!

If The Shoe Fits

THE WEEPER

The "weeper" uses the
Slightest provocation
To make of each person
A "crying-station."
Real or fancied slights
Or imagined wrongs
Become the subjects
Of his mournful songs.
Sprinkled generously
With crocodile tears,
The tunes are sung
Into friendly ears.

With his misery spread
Among his friends,
The groaner's self-pity
Quickly ends.
Then on his way
He goes gaily anew,
Leaving his friends
Distressed and blue.
But to the weeper's habit
They soon get wise,
And meet with a grin
The next sad cries.

The World Is Your Mirror

ENDURANCE OR APATHY?

Patience,
In the face of adversity,
May be a virtue;
But inaction,
In the face of wrong-doing,
Is a vice.

SECRET OF SURVIVAL

It is one of nature's strangest paradoxes
That to live one must sometimes kill;
And so it is
That to prevent a slow death by attrition,
From permitting one's self to be
Gnawed and nibbled away bit by bit,
One must identify,
Isolate, and cut out that offender.
For only
By destroying the threat to life
Can life for long survive.

A TOUCHY TALE

Take the bull by the horns
And you can control him;
Grab him by the tail,
And you're at his mercy.

If The Shoe Fits

THE RELUCTANT PILOT

A man is buffeted
By the tides of circumstance,
The stormy winds of chance,
And the swirling, enigmatic,
Ever-changing seas of life.
But, he ceases to be
An aimless drifter,
A tempest-tossed bit of flotsam,
When he stands firmly,
Rational and decisive,
At the helm of his own sturdy craft.

GYMNASIUM

The far-sighted and hopeful mind
Views present problems
As instruments to condition
Mental muscles
And build up strength of spirit.

PICK 'N CHOOSE

Be open minded enough
To see another's style of life
May be just his size,
And independent enough
To design and develop your own
To a similarly
Comfortable fit!

The World Is Your Mirror

THE ANSWERED PRAYER

Two strangers praying
Knelt side by side.
As they rose to leave
One seemed dissatisfied
And complained
That his requests
Were seldom granted.
His neighbor smiled
And answered in this way:

"True it is that
Some prayers are answered
And some seem to go unheard.
But, could it be
That most answered prayers
Are those which do not ask
For God to work alone?"

When we do more
And ask for less,
Our lives are often
More fully blessed.

OVERKILL

Some who are willing to work
Very long and very hard
To achieve a goal
Are, then, unwilling to stop
Quickly enough or long enough
To enjoy it.

THE DREAMERS

Consult your history books
And carefully assess
Some dreamers who attained
Enduring success.

Clinton, Whitney and Howe
Had much laboring to do,
As did Fulton and Bell,
To make dreams come true.

The work-lamps burned
Far into many a night
For McCormick and Ford
And the Brothers Wright.

Morse, Eastman, Marconi,
And Mister Edison, too,
Knew dreams were not enough —
That there was work to do.

Einstein struggled for years,
As did Pasteur, the Curies —
For advancements in science
To serve humanity.

There are two kinds of dreamers,
I'm sure you'll agree:
Those who act upon their dreams,
Those content with fantasy.

The World Is Your Mirror

THE MAGIC WAND

Do not sit sadly
By the cinders of an evening,
Sighing in your heart
That your life is dreary,
Your talents meager,
Your ambitions directionless
And your dreams unattainable.

For with the magic wand of faith,
Belief in yourself
And in your ability to achieve,
You can turn your tattered rags to silk,
The mice of timidity to horses of courage,
And the pumpkin of despair
To a coach of confidence.

For such faith
Will release the necessary energy
And inspire the determination
To carry you relentlessly
To the castle of your dreams.

PARTIAL STARVATION

Many are careful of their diets
To supply the body's need
But fail to give souls and minds
Things on which they feed.

THE ORCHARD BORE

Experiences,
Like fruit, often ripen
At a certain season,
And ought then be harvested,
Tasted and savored.
For in time
Their richness
And flavor wanes,
And the opportunity
To enjoy them
Is forever lost.

KITTY

She purrs so sweetly to his face
And hails him with that feline grace;
But whenever he is not around
She hisses, claws and tears him down.

She tells me he's selfish and so unfair,
While praising me for understanding rare.
But I begin to wonder uncomfortably
How, in my absence, she may speak of me.

THE CLUTCHING HAND

One's grasping for material wealth
May be inspired initially by dire need
But, after success, that pursuit is sustained
By the insatiable lust of simple greed.

The World Is Your Mirror

NOT FOR EXPORT

Piling up laurels and dollars
Seems to know no end;
Yet no one has found how to take them
Beyond the Bend.

That "you can't take it with you"
Should cause you no worry or pain;
To live fully and contentedly
Should be life's greatest aim.

You can't take it with you
When the Road of Life ends,
So make the most of what you have
While you're living, friends!

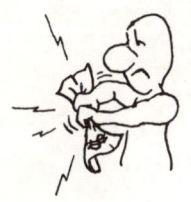

THE SQUEEZERS

Some people squeeze a dollar
So hard
There's no juice of pleasure
Left in it.

WHOLE OF HEART

It is not the envied
Who are most contented
But those without envy.

If The Shoe Fits

THE GREATEST MAN IN THE WORLD

He's not that much to look at,
He isn't all that strong.
But in her eyes, quite plainly,
He's special and does no wrong.

He's John Doe—no world shaker,
And won't ever make President.
But he's the big man with her,
She's sure he's heaven-sent.

He's hardly the life of a party,
His friends don't think him a wit,
But he fills her life with gladness
And keeps the flame of her love lit.

To the world that passes by him,
He is "Clark Kent" at best.
But when he comes home for the evening
She sees an emblazoned "S" on his chest.

To her he's as mighty as Samson,
As suave as Cary Grant,
As wise as the fabled Solomon,
As funny as Charley's Aunt.

For the thing she continues to see in him
Is the happiness he's brought to her life,
Although this greatness has gone unnoticed
By everyone, except his wife.

The World Is Your Mirror

MAJOR RESOURCE

Whenever tempted to sacrifice
Time or principle for pelf,
It's well to realize one's
Major resource is one's self.

Too much store may be put
In material goods and wealth,
On treasures locked in vaults,
Or placed upon a shelf.

One's self contains the potential
Of what one can be—
And is one's major resource,
Won't you agree?

ALL THAT GLITTERS

We struggle so desperately
For some things in life,
And once we achieve them
We find out how trivial
Many of them really are.

T(A)INTED LENSES

How often man's view
Of honesty
Is colored by the
Possibility of gain!

If The Shoe Fits

THE UNGUARDED MOMENT

The best guide
To a person's
True character
Is to observe him
When he is making
A moral decision
In an unguarded moment.

When he feels that
His reputation is not
Under scrutiny,
Then his true character
Will assert itself
Openly, freely.

Hold precious
Those friends
Whose character
And reputation
Will stand the test
Of the unguarded moment.

THE CLINCHER

It makes for a sorry state
When one can convince
Even the closed-minded,
Cajole the ornery,
And con the gullible
Into almost any action—
If he can persuade them
That it will be
Personally profitable.

The World Is Your Mirror

MAHOMET

He is half way there
Who realizes that his goal in life
Will not come to him,
That, instead, he must reach it
Primarily under his own power.

SANDPAPER PERSONALITIES

Some people seem
To have an uncanny knack
For making the most
Ill-suited cracks.

They rub the wrong way,
Though smiling and sunny;
And they grate even worse
When they try to be funny!

A few are just rude,
Unregenerate bores;
And these we can only
Avoid or ignore.

GLUG! GLUG!

Some who begin on the bottom floor
Get just that far and then no more
For self-pitying blues from their mouths so pour
Drowning out opportunity's knock at their door.

SCIENTIST OF THE SIXTIES

His eyes roll while the test tubes bubble,
And he doesn't anticipate any trouble
As he rubs his hands after hours of toil,
Watching his formula rise to a boil.

He's positive he's found it, found it at last—
A mouthwash that drives bad breath away fast.
He rushes to try it as quick as can be,
So they can start plugging it on TV.

He takes a swallow—breath's fresher, no doubt,
Mouth's definitely cleaner—his teeth just fell out.
So, back to the drawing board for success athirst,
But next time he'll do more experiments first.

WHY IN THE WIDE WORLD?

Some women will wear the pants
For which they've not the end,
And so discourage much romance
By following mere fad or trend.

WHOSE HAND AT THE WHEEL?

In a world of constant motion
Man must, also, always move;
His worthiness to challenge
He must continually prove.
In a world that ever changes
A man cannot stand still;
And if he won't direct his footsteps
There's always someone else who will.

The World Is Your Mirror

WHEN WORLDS BEGIN TO TOPPLE

When I was a child
And my castles tumbled,
I thought the world
Was coming to an end.

When I was a youth
And lost my first love,
I thought I'd never know
A deeper agony.

As I moved forward in life
Suffering Fortune's knocks,
Often I felt my universe
Shudder and tremble.

Now I know scorched fields
Can grow green crops
And that one's struggles
Build a strong heart.

So today, I look Life in the eye
And say with a smile:
"I've licked problems before
And I'll lick them again!"

27

If The Shoe Fits

EYES OF AVARICE

Too many claim
As their natural right
The objects of
A gluttonous appetite.

GIBRALTAR

Like a firm and sturdy rock
Amid the turbulent raging sea,
A man possessed
Of inner strength and calm
Is most capable of surviving himself
And helping others towards hope
In times of strife and turmoil.

PERILOUS POINT

It's dangerous when one
Comes to feel he has nothing to lose;
For he may sacrifice integrity
And discard self-respect.

FANCY FIDO

One who constantly
"Puts on the dog"
Usually ends up
In other people's doghouse.

The World Is Your Mirror

NO ACCOUNT

Many who believe that
The world owes them a living
Are bewildered
When they discover,
That their lives are bankrupt.
They don't realize that
The world, like any other bank,
Only pays dividends
On something invested.

THE PRODDERS

Sometimes our harshest critics
Help us more toward improving ourselves
By pointing out our weaknesses
Than do our loyal and devoted friends
By quietly tolerating them.

YOUR RIGHT HAND

When someone wants to be
Your right hand,
Be certain your left hand
Knows what your right is doing.

DANGERS OF A DRAWBRIDGE

Automatically raising
Our emotional defenses
To deflect
Another's sheer logic
May cut us off
From reality itself.

If The Shoe Fits

SMART FISH!

Excessive ambitions
Sometimes tempt
"Smart" humans to step
Beyond their element.

Lacking necessary strength
To survive the new fold,
They leave themselves open
To frustration and cold.

The poor fish, according to
Its strength and size
Will find and keep within
Its own level. How wise!

Oh, to be as smart as a fish!

HISTORY LESSON

Those tyrants
Who'd devour the world
Should be aware
That all who have tried
Have, in the end,
Choked on it!

The World Is Your Mirror

IF IT HURTS ENOUGH!

Touching a hot stove
Teaches a lesson rough
To those who are burned—
If it hurts enough!

Hurt can arouse the spirit,
And in the mind and soul
Create the dynamic force
For attaining a goal.

When failures hurt deeply
Our energies are fanned
To control the situation
With a determined stand.

The plague of failure
Or some sharp rebuff
Can spur one to new action,
If it hurts enough!

TENDERFOOT

A sucker who's
"Taken for a ride"
May suffer most
From his hurt pride!

If The Shoe Fits

THE DRONES

The reflex-action devotee
Will very quickly fade away
From the fad gone out of season,
For his devotion has no reason.

So, too, with such knee-jerk friends,
Their friendship very quickly ends
When, like bees, they once detect the hour
They can get more honey from another flower.

THE VELVET GLOVE

Of the "velvet glove,"
Be cautious, son;
The hand it covers
May be a gentle one,
But just as easily
It may conceal
A knockout punch
From a fist of steel!

HEE-HAW

The braying of a jackass
Betrays the absence
Of any real horse sense.

The World Is Your Mirror

PEP TALK

Now, you're the coach of this football team
And it's half-time on the field,
And as the players limp into the locker room
Your anger you can't conceal.

Your backfield has three All-Americans,
You outweigh the foe easily.
So how come you are now losing
Thirty-five to three?

Your passer is thrown for many losses
And your runners hit stone walls.
Your receivers seem always to be covered,
And your blockers are being mauled.

You tell them they'd better buckle down
Or you'll dock them all some pay.
But wouldn't it be more helpful
To give them a few new plays?

Your opponents are using the latest offense,
So you give them quite an edge
When all your team has going for it
Is the drop-kick and flying-wedge.

MOOT PURSUIT

An idea is like a woman,
You pursue it
'Til it catches you.
Then—
It drives you,
Coaxes you, controls you,
Sometimes even
Spends your money.
Yet, when you add it all up—
It still seems worth it.

METHOD IN MIND

He is successful
Who, not merely
Plans on reaching a goal,
But plans how.

SECOND WIND

Many men meet with failure,
Not because they lack
Ability to succeed,
But because they refuse
To employ their imagination
To develop new plans
When earlier ones
Have fallen short.

The World Is Your Mirror

MENU FOR BANKRUPTCY

The customer complained
That the food was
Tasteless junk.
The owner had heard
These complaints before
And called them
So much bunk!

Now the proprietor
Is sure he was right,
That what he
Had said was true.
There are no customers
Left to fight
Or to dispute
His view.

THE SPIRIT'S COMING OF AGE

A man does not begin
To grow up
Until he stops
Tearing others down.

HELPING OR HINDERING?

Carrying everyone's load
On your shoulder
May cause you to fret,
Fuss and smolder.

Are others incapable
Of the effort it takes
To do for themselves and
Make their own breaks?

Do you think they can't
Get along without you?
Someday that's what
They'll have to do!

It's best that you let them
Begin right now
To use their own hands
For guiding the plow.

Of helping themselves,
Let them have the pleasure;
The deep, rich experience
Is one they'll treasure.

Find yourself a new outlet
Your energy to employ—
Some other release
In which to find joy.

The World Is Your Mirror

I. Q. TEST

Ah, you're very shrewd!
Such a keen aptitude!
That's what I've finally decided.
For you racked your brain,
Then finally came
To the same conclusion that I did.

THEORY OF RELATIVITY

One never learns
How many relatives he has
Until they learn
How much money he has.

RETRIBUTION

While man's laws are designed
To punish abuse of another,
Nature's very surely
Punish abuse of self.

LUMPY LACTOSE

A potential source
Of human compassion and love,
The milk of human kindness,
Held miserlike in one's own heart,
Only curdles and sours
In his mind and attitudes.

THE PARENTAL CHALLENGE

It's hard to teach children filial piety
When kids on TV, who always run rioty—
And make of their parents bumbling fools,
Are thought to be cute for breaking the rules.

And how do we tell youth never to cheat
When Daddy brags of traffic tickets he beat?
And where's the percentage in keeping one's word,
With newspapers headlining the breakers' reward?

Or how do we say, and keep a straight face,
That honest, hard work will win us the race,
When riches are garnered by just pulling strings
And people are paid for not doing a thing?

Yet there is something we still can do:
To responsible principles and values be true,
So that the trusting eyes looking up to us
Will see a close example of one honest and just.

The World Is Your Mirror

COMPOUNDED INJURY

The hurts we may receive or feel
Oft spark a rage we can't conceal,
And provoke us to strike a vengeful blow
At a suspected cause of all our woe.

Yet such acts may warp or destroy our life,
And bring us just more grief and strife,
If the pain to which our wrath gives birth
Is more than the first small wound is worth.

PRAGMATIC PERIL

To attain a goal some work hard
While others will cheat or pilfer;
For both, motivation is the same,
Only their methods differ.

But a world of moral, civilized men
Will remain but an idle dream,
If, however noble or worthy an end,
It justifies any means.

BEN HUR

The road
To accomplishment,
Is most surely,
Most swiftly traveled
In a chariot pulled
By the sure-footed horses:
Imagination, Effort,
And Self-Discipline.

If The Shoe Fits

THREE STRIKES AGAINST HIM?

The oldest,
Most convenient alibi of all
That every failure
Still recalls
Is that the world
Is somehow rigged,
And that's why he
Has never made it big.

He claims he was jinxed
By life's draw,
But opportunities came
That he never saw.
Breaks went against him,
He's always cried,
Yet when he got chances,
He never tried.

How comforting to say,
After losing a game,
That society or bad luck,
Or the rules are to blame.
But how can one expect
To win anything,
If, at his turn up to bat,
He won't take a swing?

QUIET, PLEASE

If you can't be civil,
Be silent.

The World Is Your Mirror

RISK CAPITAL

If hoarded in a mattress,
Or hidden in a wall,
A penny saved is a penny saved,
And that is all.

It may keep a man from poverty,
But hardly anymore,
While investing wisely's likely
To open many a door.

For the doors to the golden chances
Rarely open to the miserly,
But often do to those who employ
Their imagination as a key.

THE THREE I'S

In the word "success"
There are invisible I's
We may number 1, 2, 3.

I'll list them so
You need not guess:
Ingenuity, Industry, Integrity.

When spelling success,
It's certainly wise
To give proper place
To those unseen I's.

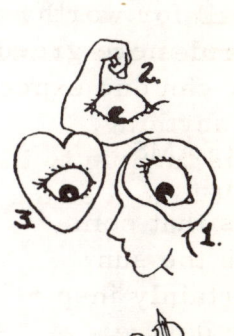

EGO-OBSTACLE

Many a man
On his way to greatness
Has been waylaid
By his own self-importance.

YOUR MOTIVES

That extra deal you had to close,
A monumental project you propose,
The seaside manor you just bought—
Just a bit bigger than a rival's got,
The pretty young gals you wine and dine
To assert you're not yet past your prime—
Is that all for worthy ambition spent,
Or to feed mere greed and soothe discontent?

DAYDREAMS

Dreams that come
Beneath the sun
Can certainly inspire
A noble desire.

But, if then, you do
Not follow through,
All of your daydreams
Will only stay dreams.

The World Is Your Mirror

I'M FROM MISSOURI

Don't make
Any rules for me
By which you
Will not yourself abide;
Don't ask me
To discharge responsibility
From which
You seek to hide.

If you'd change
My way or pace of living
Hollow preachment
Will never slow me;
But I'll note your example
And perhaps be inspired—
If you don't just tell me—
But show me!

CHARISMA

His abilities can earn one
The applause of others,
But only his warmth and sincerity
Can win their affection.

STITCHES IN TIME

No one can weave into reality
The tapestry of big dreams,
Until he's successfully mastered
The slender threads of detail.

If The Shoe Fits

TALKING TO THE WALL

Oh, why can't you understand?
It's plain as the palm of your hand.
My idea's foolproof, don't you see?
What do you mean you just don't agree?
You've got to be kidding, of course.
Or else you've not the sense of a horse.

Its wisdom is self-evident;
Just use your head as it was meant.
Of course, I've got an open mind
And will heed such ideas I may find
That're better than those I get.
Trouble is, I've not found one yet!

TOP BRASS

He looked decisions
Right in the eye,
And never even flinched.
He made up his mind,
And stuck to it,
Never gave an inch.

He took command
Immediately,
Never pondered long.
He'd have been
One of history's heroes,
But his decisions were usually wrong.

The World Is Your Mirror

CAUTION PAYS!

Of caution, high may be the price,
But even higher is the prize;
One false step is enough to send
The mountaineer to an icy end.

A split-second failure to defend
Sends a fighter down for a count of ten;
A careless move and the toreador
Gives the bull a chance to gore.

Constant caution, wise may prove,
If it prevents the one false move
That may weaken, mar, or even kill
Something that took us years to build.

THE ENVIABLE

One who has found a purpose in living
And spends his time and energy pursuing it,
Need not wonder at the meaning of life,
Nor at what place and hour its riches are found;
For he has already discovered the answer.

UNFULFILLED DESIRES

The baby, wanting something,
Cries.
A child, denied its own way,
Whines.
The unsatisfied adolescent
Pouts.
Frustrated, immature youth
Flies into a rage.
The disappointed adult may
Sulk in silent bitterness.

Fortunate is the man
Who is able to realize
That the failure
To achieve one desire
Adds luster to the
Fulfillment of others.
It's the dry, dusty throat
That most enjoys
A sudden-found spring.

CURIOSITY

Curiosity may have
Killed the cat—
But it's opened a lot of doors
For man!

PART II

MAKING STRIDES

MAKING STRIDES

We may grumble
When we stumble
As those first
Little steps we take.

We may fall, but then
We get right up again,
And each time learn
From our mistakes.

Then when we've begun
To finally run,
We see what giant strides
They helped us make.

FAIR EXCHANGE

When wondering what others
Can contribute to you —
Try weighing what you
Have to offer them, too.

THIS LITTLE PIGGY...!

Every day
Four-footed hogs
Are born in the world.
While here they accept
What they are given,
And departing,
Leave chops and hams
As a feast for others.

Not so with
Those two-footed hogs
Who demand the most,
The best.
Upon departing,
They leave nothing
But the unhappiness
They created for others.

Making Strides

I'M SORRY

Some people have a way
Of saying "I'm sorry,"
And continuing to do
The same old things
In the same old way,
As though they think
Saying "I'm sorry"
Gives them license
To repeat the offense.

FRIENDLY PERSUASION

Plant your idea
In the other fellow's mind
So that he can seize upon it
As if it is his very own.
Then let him lead you
Down your own alley
Until HE convinces YOU.

SWEETENED AIR

Smiles, like flowers,
Suddenly bloom and quickly fade;
But how long lingers
The joyous effect they made!

If The Shoe Fits

TROUBLE-HUNGRY

On trouble
Some people seem to thrive;
Unless involved in struggle
They're but half-alive.

With a battle over,
They suffer discontent
Until another problem
They can invent.

"A" FOR EFFORT

They may not be perfect
In what they do
But for sincere effort
Some credit is due.

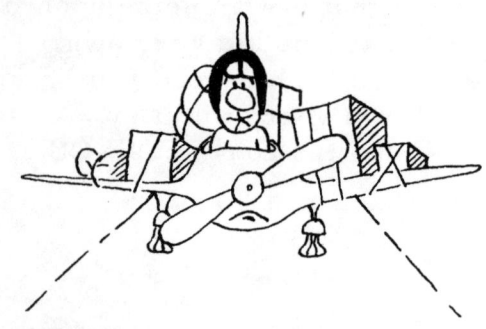

EXCESS BAGGAGE

Much of what we have
And most of what we desire
We could better get along without
And spare ourselves much concern.
Is it just being human
That we who need so little
Always want so much?

Making Strides

THE LADDER OF SUCCESS

Many people who go up
The ladder of success
Do not climb.
They are pushed, pulled,
Tugged and lifted,
Rung by rung,
Through the efforts of others.

It is little wonder they flop
When they reach the top
And have to rely
On themselves!

CONTACT

Only the spark of purpose
Can ignite the fuel
Of constructive thought
And set in motion
The engines of real progress.

PROFESSOR DUNCE

One who thinks
He can learn
Only from self
Has a fool
For a teacher.

If The Shoe Fits

LEAVE WELL-ENOUGH ALONE

Why create unnecessary problems
That make us fret and moan?
Life can be happier if we learn
To leave well-enough alone.

Why borrow others' troubles,
As a thankless sort of loan?
A double load can bring despair,
So leave well-enough alone.

Let those that cause such problems
Their sorry lot bemoan—
Let them learn, as you and I,
To leave well-enough alone!

20/20 VISION

Wise is he
Who has the hindsight
To recognize his mistakes
And the foresight to use them
Toward future successes.

Making Strides

SEEING DIFFERENTLY

From other people's mouths
Is spoken Truth they perceive,
And I find what I'm hearing
Quite hard to believe.

They say some people
Hear and see only part,
And that each will interpret
From his mind or heart.

But I was there, first-hand,
To hear and to see—
And the whole incident seemed
Very different to me.

I wonder, since our reports
So divergent be,
Who heard and saw only part—
The other person or me?

SWEET TALK

When the little lady
Starts buzzing around,
Spreading a little more
Honey than usual,
She probably has a
"Bee in her bonnet."

THE HALL OF FAME

We dust the statues
Of our honored ones
And prepare the pedestals
For those to come.
We're so certain
Who'll make our hall of fame
We'll prematurely chisel
In their names.

Yet how often we discover
Day after day
That another of our heroes
Has feet of clay,
And the promising one
For whom we saved a space
Has faded, and
A stranger now takes his place.

It's all very well
To predict the winning one,
But let's not pass out laurels
Until the deed is done.

PERFECT VISION

The ability to see
The good in others
And recognize the
Bad in ourselves
Is perfect vision.

Making Strides

FOUNTAIN OF INFANCY

What are we expected to think
Of those who claim to "need a drink"
To calm their nerves and tensions cure,
To make them feel more self-assured?
Medical science says it's true
That, in fact, the only people who
Need a bottle for security
Are children in their infancy.

WITH WISDOM SOWN

So your blossoming actions
May bear the fruit
Of a joyous and rewarding future,
Begin now by planting the seeds
Of wise and constructive thought.

NOT IN OUR STARS

So often when we do something wrong,
We seek a scapegoat to blame it on.
A "somebody gave us bad advice,"
Or "our environment wasn't nice."

But when we look in a mirror,
As eventually we must,
We find the real culprit
Looking back at us.

If The Shoe Fits

BOOBY-TRAP!

Life may be a bowl of cherries—
But even cherries have pits!

WHO LEARNS?

"One is never too old to learn,"
An old adage states;
"Can't teach old dogs new tricks,"
Another relates.

Both these old sayings
Are true in their turn—
Depending upon the individual
And his willingness to learn.

By the way, which adage
Is the one others see
When they take a look
At you and me?

Making Strides

VIRTUOSO

The mind is the artist,
The body a mere instrument
Upon which one plays
The concerto of his life.
The mood, the tempo,
The beauty or dissonance,
Are, therefore, determined
Not so much by the instrument,
As by the talent and dedication
Of the artist.

BENCH JOCKEYS

Those who say
That the road to success
Is easy,
And that most
Who reach that destination
Are merely "lucky,"
Rarely have traveled it
Themselves.

EMBRYO

The egg of a potent idea,
Fertilized by the seed of desire,
Develops and is brought into the world
To be nurtured and guided to maturity
Through dedicated efforts,
Consistent and perservering.

If The Shoe Fits

THE FERTILE SOIL

The mind is like a field of fertile soil,
Something will grow from it.
Left untended, it will produce only the wild weeds
Of aimlessness and frustration.
So, to insure a fruitful harvest,
One must sow and carefully cultivate
The seeds of useful, constructive thought.
Only then will it blossom with the
Beautiful, nourishing fruit
Of achievement, satisfaction and contentment.

THE REVELATION

Not who
We were born, nor where,
But what
We make of ourselves,
Is what
Most counts to others—
And should, also, to us.

Making Strides

BOOMERANG!

He greeted people and shook hands
Like a breeze brushing by.
When others were talking
His mind seemed far away.

He simply did not share
In other people's interests,
And soon his disinterest
Boomeranged right back at him!

THE WISE AND FOOLISH

In men who are profound and wise
There is a little foolishness,
And in the foolish man
There is a little wisdom.
But a very foolish man
Is the wise man who recognizes
Foolishness in others
But not in himself.

JUST CAUSE

Not to feed our pride
By others seeing us in good light,
But for our own peace of mind
Should we always do
What we believe is right.

If The Shoe Fits

MARDI GRAS

The person who for others
Usually dons a false-face
Has feelings and motives
With flaws some place.

The loud, hollow chuckle,
Belied by mirthless eyes,
And the supercilious air
Are elements of disguise.

Through the fawning smiles
And fake solicitude,
The penetrating viewer
Strips masked-ones nude!

FLYING BLIND

The main reason that some
Land where they do
Is that they fail to chart
Their whole flight
Before the take-off!

Making Strides

NOT-SO-BAD DEBT

Don't complain if you're not repaid,
It might be worth the loss.
If the lesson's learned, and the point made,
You may be spared later, bigger cost!

NOT LATER—BUT NOW!

That which we postpone
May never get done;
That awaited tomorrow
May never come.

DON'T-CARE-ITIS

To stand idly by
While an evil goes unchallenged
And a problem goes uncorrected
Betrays a tragic addiction
To the drug of indifference,
And a perhaps-fatal
Lack of commitment
To any principles of morality.

If The Shoe Fits

HAPPY TALK

From most conversations
There is little to gain;
They are usually recitals
Of problems and pain.

So speak of pleasures,
Of joys and of fun;
This "switch" in discussion
Will be a welcome one.

SPLASHING!

Politicians have found mud-slinging
A game two can play—
With you and me, such activity
Works the same way!

Without getting some on yourself,
You cannot splash another.
So be careful what you're splashing—
That's all, brother!

FORT KNOX

The currency of a man's word
Is worthless
Until backed up by the goal
Of proven performance.

Making Strides

PROGRESS

The real victories in life are won,
Not by those who are always
Making concessions to reality,
But by those who try to change it,
And succeed.

SHADOWS

As the darkness
Disappears
With the dawn,
So prejudices
Fade fast
With the light
Of understanding.

SELF-IMPRISONMENT

Evil thought creates
A mental prison:
Evil listened to
Becomes its bars,
Evil seen becomes
Its chains,
And evil spoken
Soon forms its lock.

POKER FACE

Do not let the austere
Countenance of pessimism
Bluff you into giving up
Just when fortune's dealt you
A winning hand.

SERVANT OR MASTER

Time—meant to be
A servant of man—
Is all too often
His master.

BRIGHTER, BRIGHTER

An inevitable result
Of widening
The beam of one's vision
Is the illumination
Of more and broader opportunities.

NO POST-MORTEMS

People who consistently
Have second thoughts
Should try improving
Their first ones.

NO TIME?

We will find time for anything
We care enough about!

Making Strides

ULTIMATE CRITERION

They can put a man
On a pedestal,
Have him admired
Far and wide;
But he'll never
Really be that tall
Unless he feels
That way inside.

The crowd can make
A man a king
And call him
A big "success,"
But he must reach
Goals he's set himself
If he's to find
True happiness.

QUICKER THAN THE EYE

The real leaders of men
Are not those with the vision
Merely to see an opportunity,
But those with the courage
To seize it.

INTROSPECTION

For every fault
One finds in others,
Self-scrutiny
Reveals two brothers.

If The Shoe Fits

WAITING FOR PROVIDENCE

The man willing to struggle
For self-improvement
Finds that others
Are eager to help him.

But the man
Who waits for Providence
To lift him out of his rut
Has a long, long wait.

TO EACH HIS OGRE

We all recognize that
Many children fear the dark—
But, it's amazing how many
Adults fear enlightenment!

KNOWLEDGE IS SECURITY

Only by learning all we can
Of what is knowable to man
Can we limit the scope
Of unknown dangers
And adequately prepare
Defense against those
Which newfound knowledge
Has revealed.

Making Strides

MUTINEER

The body may be the servant of the mind,
But it quickly rises in open rebellion,
If not forcefully and firmly subjugated,
By a self-disciplined master.

TAILSPIN TEMPO

See the man who's ruled by
Worry. Worry. Worry.
See his frantic pace; watch him
Scurry. Scurry. Scurry.
Note how favor of "big wheels" he'll
Curry. Curry. Curry.
Listen to him talk. His mind's in a
Flurry. Flurry. Flurry.
It's a collapse he's heading for in a
Hurry. Hurry. Hurry.

THE CONSTANT

To successfully cope
With the insistent pressures of life
And achieve any real peace and satisfaction,
One must learn to absorb the calmness and joy
From his moments of mental relaxation
And intellectual inspiration.
Building the quiet strength
That will maintain him through
Emotional strains and crises.

If The Shoe Fits

THE IVORY TOWER

Some sit in the castle of their dreams
And look out from the tower of their hopes,
Confident that they are protected
By the moat of aloofness
That they have dug
Between themselves and the world.
But they never stop to think
That their defenses deter,
Not only those who would do them harm,
But also those who would be their friends.

SLEEPING BEAUTY

The dormant genius in each of us
Is awakened by the kiss of inspiration
And brought into the sunlight
By the steady hand of courageous effort.

TURNING POINT

It is that moment
In the life of a man
When he begins
To understand
That if his dreams
Are to come to pass
He must stop dreaming
And begin to act.

Making Strides

STAND UP!

The man who chooses
To lie in comfort
Is at a disadvantage
When Life's battles come.
Not only is he unable
To fight back while prone,
But he's not even
In a position to make
A strategic retreat.

HOT SPOT

If you'd avoid
An uncomfortable position,
Don't let yourself
Be caught in-the-middle!

WHAT DIFFERENCE?

No one can dispute
That a good brain
Is more valuable
Than a poor one.

But who can tell
The difference
When the good one
Is not put to use?

GIFT HORSE

While it is said to be impolite
To look a gift horse in the mouth,
Don't bet on his winning you a purse
Until you've first seen him run.

HEAR, HEAR!

Even when they talk to themselves,
Some people do not listen!

BUTTON UP!

If it were as easy
To button up one's lips
As to button up one's shirt,
How much, oh, how much
Trouble could be avoided.

THE RICHEST MAN IN THE WORLD

He doesn't own castles
On the Thames or the Rhine,
He doesn't have money to burn,
But he has health
Of Body, Spirit and Mind,
And he loves and is loved in return.

Making Strides

WHAT ONE GETS

As a man sows
He is said to reap;
A man, in order to eat,
Must toil for his keep.

The rich reward
For which we all yearn
Is compensation for service
And must be earned.

So let the non-receiver
Cease to complain,
For his own lack of effort,
No doubt, is to blame!

STRATA-GEMS

Diamonds of patience,
Emeralds of effort
And pearls of wisdom,
With strength of courage
For this sterling setting
Will crown our life's quest
With sparkling success.

If The Shoe Fits

TRANQUILIZER

When my nerves are tense
And I can't rest or sleep—
For me, it doesn't work
To just "count sheep."

Peace—Calm—Quiet—Relax
Are four little words of magic;
When repeated over and over,
I find they do the trick.

REFLECTED CONSIDERATION

A little consideration
Can brighten one's day,
And give great pleasure
In more than one way.

Consideration keeps
Friendships in repair—
Makes any relationship
More solid and fair.

It's like a reflector,
Sending back its warm rays;
So for the giver, too,
Consideration pays.

Making Strides

CHANTICLEER

It's the thankless task
Of lonely birds
To herald each new dawn,
And tell a world
That clings to darkness
That the time for rest is gone.

And if the solitary cry
Brings in a troubled day,
Some will that awakening
With angry stones repay.

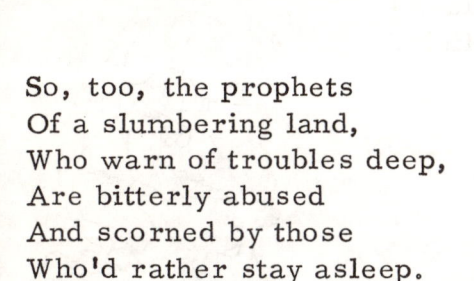

So, too, the prophets
Of a slumbering land,
Who warn of troubles deep,
Are bitterly abused
And scorned by those
Who'd rather stay asleep.

THE TREED "TIGERS"

After a single defeat
Or one tough challenge,
Some "ferocious spirits"
Are never again able
To lick anything more
Than their own wounds.

If The Shoe Fits

IF EVERYTHING WERE ALWAYS RIGHT

If life became just continuous day,
We'd weary of it soon—
Gone would be the beauty of night,
With it, the stars and moon.

If every day were sunny-bright,
There were no rain, no snow—
There'd be no Spring awakening,
And never a great rainbow.

Gone would be life's challenge,
If everything were always right—
We'd have no sense of values
And no goal for which to fight.

MOTHER LODE

More riches than have ever been mined
From the womb of Mother Earth
Have arisen from the gems to which
Man's mind has given birth.

BACKFIRE

Doomed to failure,
And better left undone
Are some tasks,
Poorly prepared
And sloppily begun.

Making Strides

POINTLESS PRESSURES

Why do some
Keep racing through life
With thrill of the chase
Obsessed,
Though now too old
To enjoy the prize
Or savor the spoils
Of conquest?

THE CONQUEROR

To win, one may make
A show of might—
But victory doesn't
Mean he's right!

AND, VICE-VERSA

One can often get a pick-up
From a let-down.

THE MOUSETRAP NOSE

What! You don't know
What a mousetrap nose is?

Why, it's a nose
That is always being caught
In the wrong places...!

If The Shoe Fits

THE WONDERS OF TODAY

"Home" was once a haven
Of rest and peace,
Where a man from his toils
Might find surcease.

Today's mechanical wonders
Allow quiet no more—
From a chorus of motors
There's a hum and a roar.

Now telephones ring,
TV and radio boom,
Groans of washers and sweepers
Come from every room.

The last payment's barely made
And one gets used to the din,
When a new gadget appears—
And it starts all over again!

Making Strides

A LA MODE

Compliments give life
Some added zest
And are most often won
By looking our best.

THE CONTRACTOR

Before a man complains to others
About life's bumpy road,
He should be certain
He didn't pave the road himself.

ALWAYS A MYSTERY

Some people expect others
To do all the work,
And never understand
Why nothing gets done.

SPECTATOR SPORT?

To even the indolent,
Work can be fascinating —
So long as others are doing it.

If The Shoe Fits

LUCKY BREAKS

A lucky break
Can make a person.
But more often
The person himself
Makes the lucky break.

THE CHIP

A chip on the shoulder
Invites a clip on the chin.

TO THE POINT

When I am not understood,
It's not my listener's fault, I fear;
Perhaps it's just that I am failing
To make myself quite clear.

EYES FRONT!

Those who look back
To yesterday
Will find only
A fading sunset,
And will miss
The bright dawn
Of tomorrow.

Making Strides

GENESIS

Fear stems
From the instinct to survive;
Hope remains
While that fear stays alive.

LIGHTNING STRIKES OUT

Opportunity can strike like lightning;
But it will not touch those
Who run from the horizon of challenge
To the shelter of simple security.

PROGENY

Brainchildren
Are essentially
Intangible beings.
But, if rightly developed,
They can have more power,
And a longer and wider
Effect on the world,
Than the men whose minds
Originally produced them.

PERSONALITY MINUS

One can win friends
With personality,
But cannot keep them
Without integrity.

If The Shoe Fits

MEMO TO A GRAY WOLF

You stand and watch the girls go by,
But never seem to catch an eye,
Your wrinkles frown, you wonder why—
Then hobble back inside.

You scan the Playboy Magazine
To learn how you can make the scene
With a shapely lass not yet nineteen,
And you are sixty-five.

The nurse comes at your helpless call
And then you chase her down the hall,
Until you stumble and clumsily fall
At your despairing doctor's feet.

Perhaps this time at last you've learned,
And to chess or shuffleboard you will turn
Or to some widow who's got cash to burn.
Now, that's more your speed.

A DELICATE BALANCE

Only a mind balanced
By the pole
Of self-honesty and patience
Can walk the precarious tightrope
Between the modesty of one's present means
And the affluence of his desires.

Making Strides

MAN'S APPETITE FOR MORE

The more one accumulates,
The greater his appetite—
Although responsibilities
Always grow less light.

When you have plenty and
Feel that craving for more,
Ask yourself if it's worth
The added headaches in store!

HAZARDOUS

Loose ends,
Things left undone,
Are often those
That trip us, son.

THE STAIRWAY TO STARDOM

Let's not complain that our part's too small,
That for any such task we stand too tall;
For many who did, when real challenge called,
We've learned were not so big at all.

Rather, play the role you're given right,
With attention, devotion, and all your might;
For 'tis then your performance may shine so bright
That expanded opportunities are brought to light.

If The Shoe Fits

PRESCRIPTION

Worry sometimes
Bogs one down,
Stamps the face
With an ugly frown,
Sours the disposition,
Sets nerves on edge,
Causes one to snap,
Whine and hedge.

There's help in music,
A hobby or book,
In dining out, or visiting
Some restful nook.
Doing something
One's wanted to do
Can change gray skies
Into blue.

No good continuing
Without a smile;
There's always something
To make life worthwhile.
Some pleasant diversion
Can one's spirit renew
And certainly brighten
A person's view.

Making Strides

MYTHING THOMETHING?

There is no such thing
As a free lunch,
An electrical banana,
Or an inexhaustible bunch.

There are no birds
With a single wing,
No rhinoceri
That soprano sing.

There are no meadows
Of chartreuse silk,
And no brown cows
Give chocolate milk.

There is no giant
Jolly and green,
No ladders into clouds
On the stalk of a bean.

And just as much a myth
As all of these be,
Is that anything worthwhile
Comes to anyone free.

TAILENDER

He who is content
Merely to ride
On others' coattails
Will always find himself
Bringing up the rear.

If The Shoe Fits

THE CLUE

A person's qualities
Are often recognizable
By a close look
At his admirers.

SOLO

There are some things in each life
One must do the way he thinks right,
And so decline offers of well-meant help
With "Please, I'd rather do it myself."

INTUITION

Intuition is
Five percent heredity,
Fifteen percent education,
And eighty percent woman.

PIGSKIN PARADE

It's good to get
A "kick" out of life,
But not by being
"Booted" around!

Making Strides

IMPULSE

Impulse is the fashion
With people of passion;
But caution, I surmise,
Is the way of the wise.

TWO OF A KIND

An idle brain,
Like idle money
Gathers
No dividends.

HUMAN DANDRUFF

Some people can get
In your hair —
Even if you're bald!

A SIMPLE SOLUTION

Giving our problems
To some of our friends
Might be a good idea,
Since the solutions
Always seem simple
To them.

THE BABBLERS

A babbling brook is restful—
A pleasure to the ear.
But when it comes to babbling people,
We'd just as soon not hear.

ANOTHER AVENUE

If one's destination is worthwhile,
But by some obstacle he's slowed,
He needn't give up the journey,
But simply try a different road.

PLUS AND MINUS

You will never correct
Your shortcomings
By dwelling upon
Your merits.

FIFTH COLUMN

It is difficult
To win the hearts of others,
If one's own has been infiltrated
By the twin saboteurs:
Bitterness and selfishness.

Making Strides

PRICED RIGHT

Free advice is
Usually worth the price!

BETTER TEACHERS

The faults and failures
Of others
Often are better teachers
Than their virtues
And successes,
For the consequences
Are more apparent.

MORE REWARDING

Forgetting another's unkind act
Is often more rewarding
Than remembering
One's own kind deeds.

PROLOGUE

Praises of thanksgiving
Best open prayers of petition
And may serve to edit the list.

A THING'S WORTH

Exotic perfumes
Begin
As odious fumes.

A horse without
Grace
Can win the race.

A moral clear
Should
Now appear:

You can't measure
Worth
By condition of birth.

BASELESS BLAST

Very often the first
To raise the roof and scream and shout
Are the last ones who really know
What they're talking about.

SMART?

A man who is smart
Is fortunate.
But, a man who thinks
He is smart
Merely because
He is fortunate
Is a fool.

Making Strides

THE NOURISHING MEMORIES

They are wise
Who gather the happy memories
Of the gay and fruitful seasons
And store them
In a corner of their hearts,
So that they may recall
And draw on them
For help and inspiration
In the barren seasons,
To sustain their outlook,
Warm their hopes
And brighten their lives.

ANYTHING BETTER TO DO?

Off yourself and your problems
You can take your mind
By thinking more often of others
In ways helpful and kind.

Thus occupied, you'll
Feel happier, too—
Is there anything better
That you can do?

RELEASE

If we'll just
Let go of our troubles,
A lot of them
Will float away!

STATE OF BLISS

One who knows it all
Can spend a lifetime
In ignorance!

HUMPTY-DUMPTY

One who always knows best
And is always right
Assumes a position
Of precarious height!

THE ONES THAT GOT AWAY

One who is always bemoaning
Opportunities that passed
Lets tears blind him to chances
That today could be grasped!

Making Strides

WITHIN EASY REACH

One looking for an argument
Sets himself a simple quest;
He needs no effort to expend
To meet with real success!

THE PASSION OF PETTINESS

Make they not a mockery of the Christ
Who fret and weep and moan
Over their petty tribulations,
Created by themselves alone?
For grudges make the heavy cross
That many people bear,
And envy is the weaver
Of the crown of thorns they wear.

BITTER-SWEET

In life's clover field
You want no bees?
Now, my friend,
Don't be funny!
Sure the bee stings
Like the devil—
But, don't forget,
He makes the honey!

If The Shoe Fits

BARK AT THE BOTTOM OF THE STAIRS

Little dogs, to show how "big" they are,
Growl and snap in a mean gruff bluff;
And "little men" yell and beat their chest
To try and prove they're big, rough, tough.
But when truly formidable challenges
Finally come their way,
Three guesses who's first to run
And which dog has his day.

MEANS TO AN END

Wisdom can find
The road to wealth,
But alas—
How rarely
Wealth finds
The road to wisdom!

AT ANOTHER'S EXPENSE

All life consists
Of rewards and penalties:
But all too many
Selfishly seek the former,
By wantonly imposing
On others the latter.

Making Strides

DO-NOTHING PHILOSOPHY

A would-be philosopher
Solemnly croaked this song:
"It is better to do nothing
Than to do something wrong."

As he spoke from his broken chair,
He rocked and fanned—
And looked out across
His parched and barren land.

PRINCIPAL AND PRINCIPLE

In business, PRINCIPAL earns
And makes interest accrue.
In society, interest is earned
By the PRINCIPLE in you!

If The Shoe Fits

ONLY THESE SHALL ENTER

My "home" is not merely
The house in which I dwell—
But my inner-self and
My environment as well.

The peace of man's castle
May come under attack
By disruptive forces
That must be turned back.

Things of love, peace and harmony
May come inside—
But admission to all others
Will be denied!

To the "homes" of others,
Consideration I'll extend—
The very same I expect
On the receiving end.

FORKED TONGUE

Insincerity
Is one of the lowest forms
Of deceit.

HERNIAL HEROISM

Many senselessly will shoulder
An unnecessarily heavy load
For the sole purpose of hearing
Their contemporaries applaud.

Making Strides

I KNOW I CAN

Like the little engine
In the fairy tale,
We chug over the mountain
Of our endeavours
Puffing, "I think I can.
I think I can."
And that's all right
For fairy tales,
But is it sufficient for us?

"I think I can,"
Means "I hope I can,"
And that means
"I'm not really sure."
The leaden pangs of doubt
Can weight and wear us down
As we chug toward
The summit of our ambitions,
So, "I believe I can"
Might bring us nearer,
But to carry us over the top
We, perhaps,
May finally have to vow
"I know I can."

NON-PARTICIPANT

No one can actually be defeated
Simply by being told "You can't do it."
For anyone who is so easily discouraged
Was never really in the game.

If The Shoe Fits

THE SPICE

Man's work is
The food of life;
Appreciation is
Its seasoning.

BITTER BACCHUS

The soul that moans
Envy's bitter song
Knows deep inside
It's he that's wrong;
But he can't improve
His own sorry shape
While drunk on the whine
From sour grapes!

SECOND EFFORT

If at first you don't succeed,
Don't give in.
For there are few initial efforts
That ever win.
But, victory comes to those with guts
To try and try again.
Yes, that second effort
Separates boys from men.

Making Strides

CAREFUL, DOC

Don't prescribe the same remedy
For every patient, please.
It may make some hale and healthy,
But just make others sneeze.

And if you're prescribing good advice,
Be just as prudent then.
For the wisest counsel is, first of all,
To allow for the differences in men.

THAT'S THE SPIRIT

Without a soul to give him life,
A man is but dust and clay;
And without action to bring it to reality,
An idea remains but a formless thought.

THE NOTHING MACHINE

Ah, what a stroke of genius!
A miracle of the mind!
Brilliant in conception,
Flawless in design.
But this fantastic new idea
Has one annoying quirk—
Each time you throw the switch on
It never seems to work.

If The Shoe Fits

THE ULTIMATE WEAPON

Wars may be waged
With arms and manpower,
But they are most often won
By the sounder strategy
And superior courage.

HAIL TO THE CHIEF

He ponders the problem thoughtfully,
Weighs each alternative carefully,
Renders his decision while timely
And stands by his choice firmly.

For the success of his efforts
And of those who follow him
Rests not only on his wisdom,
But on his strength of resolution,
As well.

PITFALLS OF A POTENTATE

One who exercises power over others
And enjoys some credit
For their achievements,
Must also be willing to accept
Some responsibility
For their mistakes.

Making Strides

WHAT'S UP, DOC?

To convince
An agile,
But independent mind,
Use,
Not the big stick
Of pressure and threats,
But the carrot
Of rational persuasion.

COMES THE DAWN!

When something-for-nothing
We grab,
We may awake to find
We "have been had."

TRACK RECORD

Follow,
Not those whose opinions
Are most showered with praise,
But those whose advice
Has, in the past,
Most often proven
To be right.

If The Shoe Fits

WHY WAIT?

You do not hobble 'round
With a pebble in your shoe.
Until your foot is aching
With blisters black and blue.

So why put off dealing
With a problem on your mind,
'Til it grows to monopolize
All your thought and time.

The man who removes the pebble
Uses wisdom and discretion,
As does he who solves the problem
Before it becomes obsession.

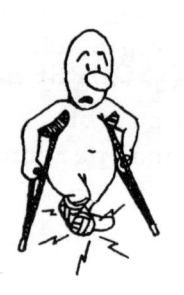

ADRIFT IN THE MAINSTREAM

Too many people plunge
Into an activity, a cause or a group
Merely to "get into the swim" of things
Without ever bothering to see
Where the current may be taking them.

THERE'LL BE SOME CHANGES

They say most people just don't change —
This truth, I begin to see;
So instead of trying to alter others,
I'll examine and try to change ME.

PART III

COUNT YOURSELF IN

COUNT YOURSELF IN

Some people insure
Their remembrance by all
Attaching names to endowments
Or to buildings tall.

But one need not be rich
To be remembered, too,
For the way he lived
And what he strived to do.

The fruits of his efforts
Can be solid and fine,
Enduring and respected
Through the test of time.

When love and humanity
Inspire his life-plan,
One lives on in the hearts
And memories of man.

If The Shoe Fits

TO EACH HIS OWN

No two sets of prints are identical
From fingers of different hands,
No two footprints make the same impression
On the shifting, restless sands.

Some prefer the bitter lemon
To the sweet sugar cane,
Some most enjoy the summer sun,
Others winter's rain.

Some men are attracted to brunettes,
While others go for blondes.
Some enjoy sailing the rolling seas,
Others float on placid ponds.

Each man decides what for himself
He likes to do and must;
And if we recognize that right in others,
They may do the same for us.

Count Yourself In

THE MOST ELUSIVE PRIZE OF ALL

We are endowed with the right
To pursue happiness,
But nowhere is it guaranteed
That we will catch it.

MEASURING UP

If, of ourselves, we demand
All that of others we ask,
We'll find our own performance
Will be equal to any task.

STATURE

When one belittles
Another man's success,
He may only succeed
In lowering himself.

MISTER JOHN HORNER

It's not how many things
One gets his fingers into—
But what they come out with
That counts!

If The Shoe Fits

WORDS

Words,
Like wine,
Should be selected
With care,
And like perfume,
Should be used
Sparingly.

INVITED GUEST

Good Fortune stops to rest
Most often on the doorsteps
To which it is invited.

ON CONDITIONS

The poor man becomes wretched
When he whines how he's abused;
While a rich one's only blessed
When his wealth is wisely used.

FAIR DEAL

You don't need
A "poker-face"
To put your cards
On the table.

RATIONAL REVIEW

How often are we agitated,
With nerves grown raw and aggravated
About some problem on our mind
Whose solution we can't seem to find.

Yet when we simply sit and relax
And calmly examine all the facts,
How easily, without our worry's help,
Does the problem seem to solve itself.

CARILLON

The bells of persuasion
Will call more to hear
And to believe one's sermons
When they peal with the ring
Of personal conviction.

UNWANTED OBLIGATION

Never put another on the spot,
Making him feel as though he's got
To return a favor that you've done.
He may resent a trap, you see;
Let his good-will come naturally,
For the only kind of friend's a willing one!

If The Shoe Fits

PRETENDED UNCONCERN

"Our birthday's just another day,"
To all our friends we say,
"And we don't expect a jot or tittle."
But if they complied and hailed us not,
Or if they just plain forgot,
We'd be hurt—and more than just a little.

THE PUPPETS

Those whose thoughts and deeds
Have little rhyme or reason
Beyond their being in style
Or it just being the season,
Who follow the crowd's consensus
And hold no belief with passion,
Will find themselves in trouble
If virtue goes out of fashion.

HELLO, SUCKER!

Contempt is the usual return
On every dollar spent
Trying to buy friendship.

Count Yourself In

MOTHER KNOWS BEST

Mother Nature watches patiently
Our every breath and move,
And wonders in a sorry way
Just what we're trying to prove.

She sees us spending recklessly
Our resources and our strength,
Without ever saving some energy
Or resting up for any length.

She permits us to defy her,
Though unfooled by our pranks.
But when we finally do collapse
We know that we've been spanked.

HOUNDED

So you feel you're being hounded
Like a fugitive or thief,
Your days are filled with anxious worry,
Your nights with restless grief.

So you run from your pursuer
In ever more weary chase,
You fill your hours with constant action
In hopes he can't keep pace.

But just once, in a fleeting moment,
You might turn and look behind.
You may discover he's but a phantom
Racing only in your mind.

If The Shoe Fits

WELL, WELL

One may have ink from a bottomless well
And quills from a thousand birds,
But not a story will he tell,
Lest his mind gives him the words.

And one can know fifty million words
And write for a thousand days,
But he'll get no attention nor be heard,
Lest he's something worthwhile to say.

THE OTHER FOOT

So, they brag about their money
And you say, "They're such bores!"
But wouldn't it be worse if they
Were trying to borrow yours?

THE CUSTOMER'S NOT ALWAYS

Do all your suggestions
Draw haughty rejections
From someone who needs what you've got?
Don't fret yourself gray,
For that's always the way
With those pretending to be what they're not.

Count Yourself In

AVARICE

Ironically,
The glitter of gold
Has put the brass
In many attitudes
And caused the tarnish
On many a life.

CEREBRAL OBESITY

Many who boast
They are broad-minded,
Are revealed in time
To be just "fat-heads."

CHUMPANZEE

See no evil, hear no evil,
Speak no evil, too;
Pay no attention to present troubles,
That's what the monkeys do.

You can close your eyes to problems
And pretend you never knew;
But, in time, untreated troubles
Will make a monkey out of you.

DUMB CLUCKS

Of the precious gift of time
Some make no better use
Than the hen who "sets"
On china eggs!

MAESTRO'S BATON

Those who were taught values and respect
To the tune of a hickory stick
Often remember the music a lot longer.

TRITE ROTE

There are few things so empty
As the perfunctory "Good morning,"
The disinterested "How are you?"
Or the thousand other phrases
Meaninglessly uttered
Only out of mechanical politeness.

They are like songs with no melody,
Just hollow, carelessly recited lyrics—
A hundred such not worth the one
Spontaneous "Glad to meet you,"
Accompanied by the music of sincerity.

Count Yourself In

KEEP MOVING

It may sound funny, but
It's all too true;
Lack of activity can
Cause stagnation in you!

If life you'd enjoy
And fulfillment find,
Keep active in body,
In spirit and mind.

Don't retire into a state
Of mental hibernation;
Get up, get around—
Keep yourself in circulation.

BUTT OUT

If it won't affect us
And is none of our affair,
And no one will be injured
Whether we do or do not care,
We can avoid the problems
Such conflicts bring about
By keeping our hands off
And our nose completely out.

SOMETHING TO CROW ABOUT

Of beating a midget
In basketball
A giant can hardly boast,
And for hurdling obstacles
Pygmy-small,
Does he deserve a toast?

Oh, he can brag
And strut through town
Showing off his prize,
But who'll be impressed
Until he's conquered
Something more his size?

COUNTER-INTELLIGENCE

Like the general,
Unbriefed on the size or strategies
Of an opposing army,
The mind that is unaware
Of the opposing side of a question
Is ill-equipped to defend its own.

TO OUR ACCOUNT

The only worldly goods we take with us
When we leave this sphere
Are the graces for the worldly good
We did while we were here.

Count Yourself In

SOMETHING MORE

Mere Good Intentions
Come to nought,
Unless brought to fruition
By Effort and Thought.

BRANDING IRON

The abuse of kindness
Marks an ingrate!

TAKING THE PLUNGE

Walking into a crowd
Of unfamiliar faces
Can be like diving
Into a pool of cold water.
While the initial splash
Is often a chilling experience,
If we stay in the swim,
We quickly find the atmosphere
Growing warmer and more hospitable.

THE TESTING

For the diamond,
Glass is just no match;
A blade of steel
Won't even scratch.
And though both
May glitter in the light,
Glass is quickly shattered
By a blow struck right.
Likewise with men,
And everything on earth:
Quality, under pressure,
Always reveals its worth.

CRAB GRASS

Ingratitude is the weed
That chokes the bright flowers
Of thoughtfulness and consideration,
And sometimes smothers
The blossoming of new opportunity.

Count Yourself In

LET THEM GROW

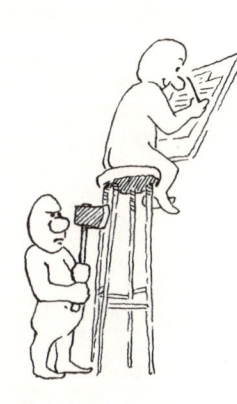

Cutting down potential giants
Never adds an inch
To the stature of pygmies.
Thus, to restrain
The gifted or the eager
So that less motivated egos
May be smoothed
Not only canonizes mediocrity,
But applies a rude brake
To the wheel of human progress.

FIRE HAZARD

By not applying more warmth
To the seat of their offspring's pants,
Parents who tolerate disrespectful children
May be playing with fire.

HELPED <u>OUT</u>!

Of those who say they'll help us out
And show us what this life's about,
Beware! Beware! Beware!
They say we need not be alone,
They'll help us manage all our own
Affairs, affairs, affairs.
But when our fortunes we have gained
That kind "helper" then will claim
A share, a share, a share.

If The Shoe Fits

THE EAGLES

The view from the top,
The admiring gaze of others
As they look into the sky
Can only be achieved
By those who bestir
Their wings enough to fly.

LITTLE SOLACE

When things go wrong,
As you warned they'd go,
Sure, you can say,
"I told you so!"

But what good does it to gloat
That your advice was best,
When you're in the same boat
And sinking with the rest?

BY CONTRAST

You can't lose what you've never had,
Feel the blues unless you once were glad,
Or flail and fret in the depths of despair
Lest the joys of hope you once had shared.

You cannot miss what you do not know,
And though the pain of loss is a bitter blow,
The memory of all past happiness then,
Gives hope it will someday come again.

Count Yourself In

THE CANNIBALS

The leeches, the parasites,
The hangers-on,
Cling to the living till
The source of life is gone.
And when they've
Drained it all away,
They leave the lifeless carcass
To float away.

And, as higher
In this world we rise,
We should beware
The vampires in disguise,
Who'll pose as friend
But bleed us dry,
Then leave us depleted,
Quite alone, to die.

TEAMMATES

The silver rhetoric of emotion
May help win an argument,
But to be meaningful
It must be alloyed with
The cold steel of logic.

DEPRECIATION

A man's integrity,
Once pawned for some temporary profit,
Can never be reclaimed
For anything near its original value.

If The Shoe Fits

THE UNSETTLING SPARK

If the presence of someone,
Or the mere mention of his name,
Triggers in us a kind of explosive fit,
It is certainly wise to keep him
Out of sight and out of mind
So our emotional fuse will not be lit.

DUPED

Many a beguiling "crusade"
Is but a wily masquerade
To which are lured the blindly naive,
Through "idealism" quite deceived,
Then manipulated like puppets of wood
In acts inimical to any common good.

STRAYING SPOUSES

Your wife, perhaps,
Seems quite a nag
And makes of your life
Such a drag
That you want to fly,
Heart in hand,
To another woman
Who will understand.
But if you carry such excursions
Afield too far,
You may encounter a husband
Bigger than you are.

Count Yourself In

A LONGER WAY UP THAN DOWN

You're on top of this old world now,
You made it up here somehow,
But you wonder what will become now
Of the thing you've found.

You were so sure you could do it,
There seemed just nothing to it,
But now that you've been through it,
You feel quite unwound.

It's all so big and faster,
And you're not sure you can master
All the rivals that come after
And surround.

But you must keep on believing,
Must keep striving and achieving,
Lest your long road of upward weaving
Be much shorter down.

If The Shoe Fits

YOUTH IS YOURS

How can one recapture youth?
Is asked every day.
It's better to retain it—
Not to let it slip away!

Keep young in hopes, in spirit,
In vision—and you'll find
Passing years cannot rob you
Of Youth you keep in mind.

THE SHOW-OFF
To flaunt one's earthly blessings
In a manner crude and coarse
Neither makes honorable use of them,
Nor honors much their source.

THE SCOREKEEPER

It is TIME
That evaluates one's qualities,
Weighs his successes,
And then
Chalks up the score!

Count Yourself In

BEAUTY OF SOUL

Beauty is ascribed to things
By individual taste —
But most can be destroyed,
Or by time, laid waste.

The one great beauty
That shines forever whole
Is possessed by the person
With beauty of soul.

PREREQUISITE

There will be no light of hope in the streets
Unless it first flicker in the hearts of men;
And no riches will imbue the outward land
Till men become first enriched within.

FAINT HEART

Those who say only
That it can't be done
Very often come to find
The race and the prizes
By others won
While they get left behind.

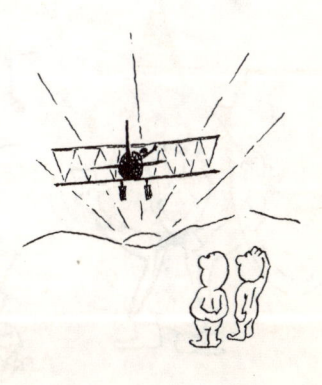

If The Shoe Fits

FUTURITY

A change of pace
May lose a race,
But prove the deed
That saves the steed
Insuring winner's pay
On yet another day.

HARMONY

As in music, so in life—
The drum is better with the fife.
Though sweet the tune, a melody
Is richer far with harmony.

A successful maestro one will be,
If he turns discord into symphony;
With many instruments employed,
A fuller life may be enjoyed.

Count Yourself In

GIFTS

A gift may well fill a need,
Bring delight and a smile—
But it's the thought with it
That makes a gift worthwhile.

A thoughtful word may be a gift
To one depressed or blue.
The gift of honor and respect
Is one cherished, fine and true.

BEGIN COUNTING NOW

"Count your blessings" is a phrase
That's all too commonly used,
In a manner so off-handed that
Its true meaning is abused.

But if one sincerely looks about,
And of his store takes measure,
He'll be amazed at the many things
That comprise his rich treasure.

Begin counting now—the job is big,
This listing of the things you've got.
No time will be left to worry or fret
About the things that you have not.

If The Shoe Fits

THE TWO SIDES TO EVERY STORY

There are two sides to every story,
But we should also remember
That, in many cases,
One side is right, and the other wrong.
And we will be far wiser if,
Beyond recognizing the two sides,
We can distinguish one from the other.

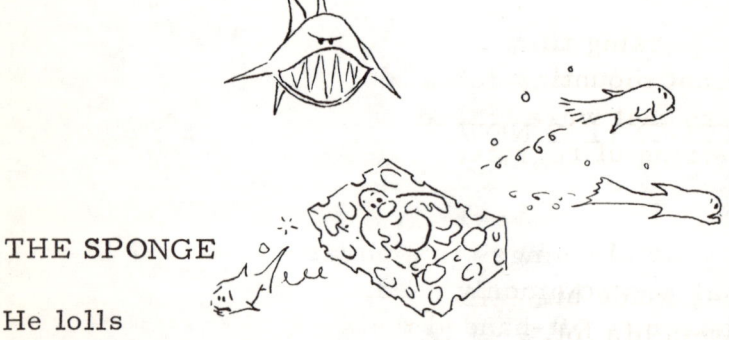

THE SPONGE

He lolls
At the bottom of an affluent sea,
Abdicates all personal responsibility,
And waits to be fed by the surging tide
And be chauffeured by a dolphin
When in need of a ride.

He sees
No need to worry, he has not a care,
For he'll let these others provide his welfare.
But when danger threatens
And all others flee hence,
He's the first one devoured,
For he has no defense.

Count Yourself In

THE MEASURE OF CREDIT

Equal opportunities
Two men had.
For one his present means
He believed so bad
That he borrowed from tomorrow
More and still more
Until he had depleted
His future store.

For him passing time
Only meant mounting debts
And years that were traced
With a string of regrets.

The other made himself
Live within his lot,
And his goal of "someday"
He never forgot.
Anticipating the future
Gave him much pleasure,
But he resisted temptations
To draw on its treasure.

When he finally reached the future
He'd been working toward,
He found worth the waiting
All its rich rewards.

If The Shoe Fits

WHAT WILL THE NEW YEAR BRING?

With the Old Year's passing
Whistles blow and bells ring;
In our hearts and minds we ask:
"What will the New Year bring?"

At this hour another question
Is the truly vital thing:
What will we, you and I,
To the New Year bring?

Of our blessings and resources
We should take stock—
And resolve to utilize those hours,
Fast ticked-off by the clock.

When this New Year becomes Old,
Then we'll have cause to smile—
If we have used this time wisely
Building a life worthwhile.

PERSEVERANCE

Those who can survive
The disappointments
Of temporary defeat
Both earn and deserve
The rewards of
Ultimate victory.

Count Yourself In

FORGOTTEN RICHES

Our daily lives are enriched
By many simple things
That may be old, but tried and true.

Yet how many fail to pause
And appreciate these—
They're too busy seeking things new!

HAPPY HUNTING

His bow was made of
Fine, sturdy character,
Strung with happiness,
And waxed with goodness.

The arrows that he used
Were made of thoughtfulness,
Feathered with generosity,
And tipped with joy.

His pull was strong and steady,
His arrows flew straight and true,
Always finding their mark—
A carefully-chosen target.

If The Shoe Fits

THE HUMAN HARVEST

Abundantly productive,
The arid desert blooms,
Barren fields grow green—
Responding to the farmer's care.

The dedicated one who tills
The fields of humanity
May stimulate lives and minds
To be vibrant, rich and productive.

Both these "farmers"—
For their worthwhile efforts—
Reap bountiful rewards
Of accomplishment.

IN BONDAGE

One who is chained
By the demands of the flesh
Is unable to embrace
The rewards of the spirit.

Count Yourself In

YOU HAVE TO BE GOOD TO STAY THERE

You have reached the top,
A place in the sun,
Crowning with success
The race you've run.

You grasped the chance,
Determined to dare,
Attaining this plateau,
Honestly and fair.

Though sweet is victory,
You've only begun;
Now comes the test—
To keep the place won.

It demands extra effort,
And constant care,
Continuous improvement,
For you to stay there!

UNDEFEATED CHAMP

Sometimes it's wiser to retire,
Able to retain our laurels,
Than to be knocked out
And have them wrested from us.

TWO-WAY DEAL

It's understandable
That most people feel
Consideration should be
A two-way deal.

But, special consideration
Some demand—
In every instance
And from every hand.

It's hard to understand
Why they are this way;
But attention feeds their egos,
And for this, friends must pay.

Inconvenience to others
Means not a thing;
Denied special attention,
Reason seems to take wing.

Though they have some virtues
This fault to atone,
One may find it wiser
Just to leave them alone!

IDLE CAPITAL

He has intelligence
And talent to burn,
But he lacks ambition
And refuses to learn.

Count Yourself In

THE DREAM PEOPLE

They walk amid our dreams at night,
The ones we think would be just right,
Who'd fill our every wish and prayer,
Who'd always serve and always care.

The fair young queen, the handsome king,
Our life, our love, our everything,
But, like the stars that fade at dawn,
They disappear when the night is gone.

And in the daylight of reality
The only ones we ever seem to see
Are imperfect people with separate souls
Who don't quite fit our ideal mold.

But we'd be wiser and happier by far
To accept them just for what they are,
To appreciate what they have to give
And love them for the way they help us live.

It's better to hold someone who's alive and warm,
Than some perfect dream that fades each morn.

JOCKEY-MOXIE

People, like some race horses,
Often are more stimulated
To reach the winner's circle
By the gentle hand-ride
Of encouragement,
Than by the stinging whip of abuse.

131

If The Shoe Fits

THIS I KNOW

If I know little else in life,
I KNOW THAT I AM HERE!
I know I did not
Cause myself to be;
A greater Force than I created me.

When help I need with problems,
Day or night,
I call upon that Power
To set me right.

I will, in my own simple way,
Bare my soul and thoughts
For Him to see,
And pray to Him to show the way,
For I am part of the Power
That created me.

Faith will give the strength
And the courage that I need,
And added wisdom bring
To mind and heart—
For of that Power
That created me,
I know that I am part.

Count Yourself In

THE GOOD LIFE

Some say it's living in stately mansions
That gaze out across the sea,
For others it's a cave or a desert isle
Where no one else would be.

Some believe it's to gain first place
In any kind of "rat race,"
Or at one's whim to grin or to glower
From exalted positions of political power;

Or to move in such an aura of fame
As to set one's fans to screaming,
Or to roam the world living adventure
Instead of just wishing and dreaming.

But the "good life" remains a fantasy
That fills men's dreams and thoughts,
And isn't it strange that so often it seems
To be what someone else has got?

TOO OCCUPIED

One who does
All the talking
Has little chance
To learn.

If The Shoe Fits

THE GOLD CUP

Like a golden cup that lies
Before the eager runner's eyes,
Each man's life should have some prize
That he is striving for.

For in order to really do his best,
A man must pass some kind of test;
Or he'll just sit around and "rest,"
And nothing more.

For without motivated thought or deed,
A man is likely to go to seed
Or fade like the poorest of the breed
And be ignored.

So, like the prize in a gold-cup race,
One's goal in life must spur his pace
And help him reach that eminent place
Where the prize is stored.

Count Yourself In

AN AMERICAN'S PRAYER

In this Year of Grace,
Dear God, we pray—
Bless our country;
And from day to day,
Let us work together
For common good,
Forging lasting ties
Of brotherhood.

With loving care,
Our way please light,
And guide us
Always in the right.
Let factional quarrels
And strivings cease,
In the interest of
Unity, honor and peace.

Help us, Lord,
To be ever aware
Of Freedom's endowments
That we share.
Make us a strong
And determined band,
In preserving the principles
Of GOD and the Land.

Amen.

Call-Enterprise and Herald American Newspapers

BETH Looks at BOOKS

YOU TOO CAN WORK WONDERS

Harry & Joan Mier

The authors of "Happiness before Breakfast" and other inspirational books have now compiled a book of inspirational verse that handles such basic questions as who are you? Where are you going and why? If you know, how do you propose to get there? This book explores the workings and the potentialities of the human mind, explaining that one does not need to understand the principles of electronics to use a television set, or be able to construct an automobile in order to drive one. Similarly, the individual need not be an expert in psychology or psychiatry to use and benefit from the phenomenal powers of the mind. In her foreword, the famous TV psychiatrist Loriene Chase, says "while each essay is brief, having a unity of its own, there runs through the entire book the intriguing theme that one CAN work wonders, become what he wants to be, succeed at what he attempts to do if he sufficiently believes in himself." A worthwhile compilation, a venture into the inner self which entertains as it educates.

Dr. Edward F. Magnin,   Los Angeles Herald-Examiner

Think Positive

There are many ways of expressing a philosophy for living. Harry and Joan Mier do this very well in "You Too Can Work Wonders."

Newport News PRESS
Newport News, Virginia

A Book Of Inspirational Thoughts

YOU TOO CAN WORK WONDERS . . . THROUGH YOUR INNER POWERS! by Harry and Joan Mier.

* * *

Harry and Joan Mier combined their thoughts and efforts and put them into a wonderful and inspiring book.

Each of us need something to carry us through the trials and tribulations which we face each day. Many of the Miers' little gems of wisdom are familiar, but have not been expressed in quite this way before.

Theirs is a book, easily read and understood, which will continue to offer advice and comfort.

B. LEE SPIRES

You Too Can Work Wonders

Through your inner powers!

- ☐ THE DYNAMICS OF SELF-APPRAISAL
- ☐ DISCOVERING YOUR INNER SELF
- ☐ TAPPING YOUR INNER RESOURCES
- ☐ ATTAINING PERSONAL FULFILLMENT
- ☐ COMING TO GRIPS WITH THE PRESENT
- ☐ PLANNING & PROMOTING YOUR TOMORROW
- ☐ GAINING LIFE'S REWARDS

by HARRY & JOAN MIER

Editors: GILBERT READE & JOHN M. KELLER
Special Foreword by:
LORIENE CHASE PH.D.
Clinical Psychologist

You Too Can Work Wonders

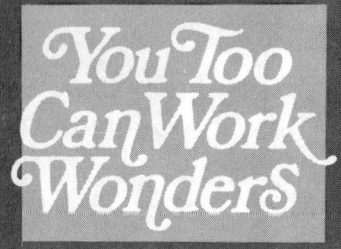

Through your inner powers!

Radio and TV personalities, commentators, public speakers and masters of ceremonies have requested and been granted permission to quote excerpts from books by the Miers:

Other books: HAPPINESS BEGINS BEFORE BREAKFAST
BUILDING OUR OWN RAINBOWS
IF THE SHOE FITS

PRE-PUBLICATION COMMENTS ABOUT THIS BOOK:

"Some books entertain, some impart new knowledge, some are fiction, some are factual. But this little volume, carefully read, can change your life, give you new courage, new expectation, new hope. It can point the way to your attainment of your highest ambition."
   Don Belding, Chairman (ret.), Foote, Cone & Belding

"'You Too Can Work Wonders' is a veritable storehouse of good common sense in capsule form, which can prove very useful in this age of confusion and hysteria."
   Dr. Edgar F. Magnin, Wilshire Boulevard Temple, Los Angeles, California

"Reading in 'You Too Can Work Wonders' excites me with the feeling that I am discovering a new constellation of scintillating insights for fulfilled living."
   Rev. Melvin E. Wheatley, Jr., Westwood Community Methodist Church

"In these tense and strange times where people, particularly the youth, have such difficulty finding a way of life, reading this book of poetic wisdom should help in bringing a feeling of self-confidence, tolerance and most important of all, a love of their fellow man and their country."
   George Jessel, Toastmaster General, Hollywood, California

SPECIAL DELUXE EDITION $1.95
(Cloth Bound $4.50)

COVER DESIGN: CHARLES BARTLESON

BUILDING our own RAINBOWS

BY HARRY AND JOAN MIER
With a foreword by Gilbert Reade

Pungent reflections on leading a life of fulfillment
by the authors of
HAPPINESS BEGINS BEFORE BREAKFAST

BUILDING our own RAINBOWS

The truth about life's foibles is viewed here with a refreshing succinctness that is never wise-acre, strutting or ostentatious. It is immediately obvious that these writers have developed their lives into something golden and inspiring. But they are realists, not romantics.

Throughout this book you will be aware of a contagious zest for people and life. The philosophy is simple: Every person has within him somewhere the ability to pull out of life genuine satisfaction.

It is virtually impossible, after reading the warm and witty jewels between these covers, to keep from making an enthusiastic beginning at your own individual rainbow.

Happiness Begins Before Breakfast

Thoughts on Life... and Living it More Fully

By Harry and Joan Mier

Edited, and with a foreword by GILBERT READE

EXPANDED EDITION

New 32-page section, "Mind Over Matter," added

SPECIAL DELUXE EDITION $1.45 (Clothbound $3.50)

Happiness Begins Before Breakfast

A LIGHT AND LOVING LIFT TO LIVING!

OVER 450 pithy prescriptions for CHASING GLOOM pages packed with wit, warmth, and wisdom!

A MENTAL-TONIC for these TROUBLED TIMES elevates spirits, brightens outlooks, evokes smiles!

No age limit...something in it for everybody!

Bright and Sunny Invitation to a Fuller, Happier Life!

Other Books *By* HARRY AND JOAN MIER
"If The Shoe Fits!"
"Building Our Own Rainbows"
"You Too Can Work Wonders"

COMMENTS ON THE WORK OF HARRY AND JOAN MIER

"...sage observations without ponderous abstractions. The pen, for the Miers, becomes another means of spreading good cheer."   —*Los Angeles Herald-Examiner*

"Happiness Begins Before Breakfast"—another instant hit! ...something in it for everybody...bits and pieces of witty, homey philosophy gleaned from a lifetime of two happy people."   —*Arizona Republic*

"The Miers revive a fine art...a treasury of truths written with kindness and humor in a modern fashion."
—*Hollywood Citizen News*

Over 300 radio and TV stations have requested and been granted permission to air excerpts from "Happiness Begins Before Breakfast."

NINTH PRINTING...OVER 200,000 IN PRINT!

BOOKS FOR THE FAMILY
BY RUTH C. IKERMAN

YOU TOO CAN WORK WONDERS: Through Your Inner Powers! by Harry & Joan Mier.

It is not easy to write a 200-page book concerning "The Dynamics of Self-Appraisal" and "Planning and Promoting Your Tomorrow," using couplets, quatrains, and other verse forms, with sometimes two or three poems on a page.

Yet this is accomplished with sustained interest by this local husband and wife writing team whose book is edited by Gilbert Reade and John Keller. The special foreword is by Dr. Loriene Chase of Santa Monica.

Some of the choice philosophy is given in bits of idiom, and one of the most pertinent is the new "Beatitude" where the authors comment "Blessed are they who are tall in spirit, for they possess the foresight and vision to see beyond accepted horizons and possibility." For all such readers this book has much to offer in the way of practical benefits.

"QUOTE" BOOKS and UNQUOTE
by EDWIN T. GRANDY

San Francisco, Calif.
Progress
Parkside Edition

"YOU TOO CAN WORK WONDERS" by Harry and Joan Mier: "Look up, look ahead, look young, feel cheerful, feel alive, feel young!" Cheerful uplift for these cheerless times.

Sacramento BEE
Sacramento, California

YOU TOO CAN WORK WONDERS by Harry and Joan Mier:

Who are you? Where are you going and why? If you know, how do your propose to get there?

These basic questions concerning the human experience provide the framework by this work of a husband-wife team.

There seemed to the Miers, they say, a definite need for a clear simple translation of the findings of scientific research exploring the workings and potentialities of the human mind in a language comprehensible to the layman.

In their book, through the Miers' observations, analyses and exposition, they set out to demonstrate that by simply recognizing the principles of cybernetics at work in the human mind and then consciously applying them, a person may achieve a deeper, more meaningful, more rewarding life.

—D. H.

MERIT *Publishers* • P. O. Box 1344 • Beverly Hills, Calif. 90213

MAIL ORDER FORM

Please send the following books by Harry & Joan Mier:

SPECIAL PAPERBACK

Title		No. of Copies	AMOUNT
Happiness Begins Before Breakfast .... 144 pages, $1.45			
If The Shoe Fits .... 144 pages, $1.45			
You Too Can Work Wonders .... 240 pages, $1.95			

DELUXE CLOTHBOUND (Gold-stamped)

Happiness Begins Before Breakfast .... 144 pages, $3.50			
If The Shoe Fits .... 144 pages, $3.50			
You Too Can Work Wonders .... 240 pages, $4.50			
Building Our Own Rainbows .... 136 pages, $2.95			

★ **INSURANCE & POSTAGE**
★ On single copy to any one address, add 35¢.
Additional copies to same address, add 10¢ each.
(This applies to each separate address)

Total Price of Books
Calif. orders add State Sales Tax
Plus Shipping Charges
Total Amount Enclosed:

_____
(Date)

PLEASE PRINT

Ordered by: _____

Address: _____

City, State, Zip: _____

MERIT *Publishers* • P. O. Box 1344 • Beverly Hills, Calif. 90213

MAIL ORDER FORM

Please send the following books by Harry & Joan Mier:

SPECIAL PAPERBACK

Title		No. of Copies	AMOUNT
Happiness Begins Before Breakfast .... 144 pages, $1.45			
If The Shoe Fits .... 144 pages, $1.45			
You Too Can Work Wonders .... 240 pages, $1.95			

DELUXE CLOTHBOUND (Gold-stamped)

Happiness Begins Before Breakfast .... 144 pages, $3.50			
If The Shoe Fits .... 144 pages, $3.50			
You Too Can Work Wonders .... 240 pages, $4.50			
Building Our Own Rainbows .... 136 pages, $2.95			

★ **INSURANCE & POSTAGE**
★ On single copy to any one address, add 35¢.
Additional copies to same address, add 10¢ each.
(This applies to each separate address)

Total Price of Books
Calif. orders add State Sales Tax
Plus Shipping Charges
Total Amount Enclosed:

_____
(Date)

PLEASE PRINT

Ordered by: _____

Address: _____

City, State, Zip: _____

(TO REMOVE — CUT OR PULL)

RADIO STATIONS BROADCAST PRAISE FOR

BOOKS BY

HARRY & JOAN MIER

YOU TOO CAN WORK WONDERS
HAPPINESS BEGINS BEFORE BREAKFAST
IF THE SHOE FITS * BUILDING OUR OWN RAINBOWS

"Amusing, interesting, and thought provoking"
WBIW, Bedford, Ind.

"Your remarks are right to the point - - excellent comments on life."
KDB, Santa Barbara, Calif.

"These books add spice and wit to our programs."
WDUN, Gainesville, Ga.

"Just delightful thoughts, so appropriate for all occasions."
KILO, Grand Forks, N.D.

"Delightful, timely, and inspirational!"
WCOA, Pensacola, Fla.

The Golden Rule in practice
As we live from day to day
Will bring us real contentment
And for others light the way.

THOUGHTS TO DELIGHT, INSPIRE AND HELP YOU TOWARD SUCCESS AND PERSONAL FULFILLMENT.

Books by Harry and Joan Mier

		Clothbound	Paperback
Happiness Begins Before Breakfast	144 pages	$3.50	$1.45
If The Shoe Fits	144 pages	$3.50	$1.45
You Too Can Work Wonders	240 pages	$4.50	$1.95
Building Our Own Rainbows	136 pages	$2.95	....

AVAILABLE THROUGH LOCAL BOOKSELLERS

Or Order by Mail:
MERIT *Publishers* • P.O. Box 1344 • Beverly Hills, Calif. 90213

Lithographed in U.S.A. — American Offset Printers, L.A.

About the Authors

Doctor Joan Gelb Mier holds the degree of Doctor of Law. The Helping Hand of Los Angeles, Inc., which helps support the Cedars-Sinai Medical Center, has honored her as the "Mother of the Year". One of ten children, she put herself through law school. As an attorney, she was especially active in legal assistance to war veterans and their dependents. She knows what effort it takes to accomplish one's goals.

Harry Mier is, in the best sense, a self-made man. From his first job as a paperboy he rose to become a pioneer in the development of one of the world's largest and most glamorous cosmetics enterprises.

Joan and Harry Mier

In a full lifetime of rich and varied experiences, Harry and Joan Mier have had vast opportunity to observe human nature in all walks of life. These experiences, like their travels throughout the United States and many countries of the world, have done much to shape their philosophy and to inspire many of the observations recorded in this volume.

Throughout the years the Miers have devoted much of their time to various civic and community projects. They have served on the boards of hospitals and welfare groups and have also been active in fraternal and service organizations.

Through their non-profit Harry and Joan Mier Foundation, they established Camp Hess Kramer on a 110-acre site near Malibu, California. The camp's wide and varied program is aimed at enriching the community's youth and encouraging good citizenship.

More recently, the Miers founded another oceanside camp, a low-altitude haven designed for crippled children further handicapped by cardiac and respiratory conditions. Donated to the Crippled Children's Society of Los Angeles County, this special facility is known as Camp Joan Mier.

In recent years the Miers have turned their talents to still another activity to become authors, gaining an ever-expanding audience with such widely-acclaimed books as "If The Shoe Fits," "Building Our Own Rainbows," and "Happiness Begins Before Breakfast." Now their fourth book, "You Too Can Work Wonders," has been added to the impressive list of delightful books by the Miers.